Greyh STYle

A Greyhound's thoughts on tackling the many ladder-stiles of Snowdonia

Pictured by Rosalie Bissell
Archie's thoughts transcribed by his Muvva, Sue Hughes.

Me, Archie!

Introdogtion

Me naym bees Archie an I'z a 'tired greyhound.

We duz lotz ov nice warks sins moovin to Wales but dem styles juss keep sketting in da way.

Hears me book ov getting ova styles da eesy way.

Me greyhound fartz carry me
hup hup an away

I'z snot brokid down, ewe nose

Rockit man burnin owt his
fuse hup here halone

Iz a fire starter,
twisted fire starter

Iz a lumberjak an I'z hokay

Muvvaz first aid practises

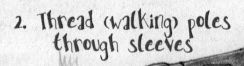

2. Thread (walking) poles through sleeves

1. Turn sleeves inside coat

Da majik of da greyhound
(an a wizzurd)

Beem me up Spokk

On a wing an a praya ov da
big burdy

Den wan day I has me crownin momunt wen I dun jumpin a stile wiv no elp.

An now I does do it al da time.

Me an me Muvva

Fank roo fur reedin me book.
Archie xx

Acknowledgements

Archie's thoughts have been inspired by:
p10, Rocket Man, 1972 . Writtten by Elton John
and Bernie Taupin.
p12 Firestarter, 1996. Writtten by Kim Deal, Anne Dudley,
Keith Flint, Trevor Horn, Liam Howlett, J.J. Jeczalik,
Gary Langan and Paul Morley.
p14 the Lumberjack Song, 1975. Writtten by Terry Jones,
Michael Palin, and Fred Tomlinson.

layout and prepress Patricia Moffett
www.patriciamoffett.com

Dedication

All proceeds from the sale of this book go to
Greenacres Rescue, Ebbs Acres Farm, Talbenny,
Haverfordwest. SA62 3XA

www.greenacresrescue.org.uk

Greenacres is sanctuary for the animals it opens its doors
and hearts for. Many animals have been subjected to extreme
cruelty, abandonment and neglect, and Greenacres dedicated
staff and volunteers set to work immediately in order to bring
the animals back health and happiness.

Some of the animals that come to Greenacres can not be
re-homed, and therefore become part of the surroundings.
Greenacres is more than a sanctuary for some, it is quite
literally their forever home.

Thank you for your donation through buying this book.